It's Ramadan and Eid al-Fitr!

by Richard Sebra

BUMBA BOOKS™

LERNER PUBLICATIONS ◆ MINNEAPOLIS

Note to Educators:

Throughout this book, you'll find critical thinking questions. These can be used to engage young readers in thinking critically about the topic and in using the text and photos to do so.

Lerner Publications Company
A division of Lerner Publishing Group, Inc.
241 First Avenue North
Minneapolis, MN 55401 USA

For reading levels and more information, look up this title at www.lernerbooks.com.

Library of Congress Cataloging-in-Publication Data

Names: Sebra, Richard, 1984– author.
Title: It's Ramadan and Eid al-Fitr! / by Richard Sebra.
Description: Minneapolis : Lerner Publications, [2017] | Series: Bumba books—It's a holiday! | Includes bibliographical references and index.
Identifiers: LCCN 2016005894 (print) | LCCN 2016007031 (ebook) | ISBN 9781512414288 (lb : alk. paper) | ISBN 9781512414998 (pb : alk. paper) | ISBN 9781512415001 (eb pdf)
Subjects: LCSH: Ramadan—Juvenile literature. | Eid al-Fitr—Juvenile literature. | Fasts and feasts—Islam—Juvenile literature.
Classification: LCC BP186.4 .S33 2017 (print) | LCC BP186.4 (ebook) | DDC 297.3/62—dc23

LC record available at http://lccn.loc.gov/2016005894

Manufactured in the United States of America
1 – VP – 7/15/16

Expand learning beyond the printed book. Download free, complementary educational resources for this book from our website, www.lerneresource.com.

Table of Contents

Holy Month

Muslims have a calendar

based on the moon.

Ramadan is the

ninth month.

It is a holy month.

Ramadan is not one day.

It lasts the whole month.

Families get together to pray.

Muslims have a holy book.

It was written long ago.

It was written during Ramadan.

People fast during Ramadan.

They do not eat or drink during the day.

How might fasting change your day?

Muslims say prayers every day.

They kneel on rugs when they pray.

They add special prayers during

Ramadan.

After sunset it is time to eat.

Fresh fruit is popular.

So is cheese and bread.

Eid al-Fitr is the last day

of Ramadan.

Fasting is over.

People eat a big meal.

Many people eat dates.

Why might people eat a big meal on Eid al-Fitr?

dates

17

The end of Ramadan is

a big celebration.

People have festivals.

Some people give gifts.

Why might people give gifts at the end of Ramadan?

Ramadan is a time
to celebrate faith
with family.

Ramadan Dates

Ramadan falls on different dates every year.

2016	June 6 to July 5
2017	May 27 to June 24
2018	May 16 to June 14
2019	May 6 to June 3
2020	April 24 to May 23
2021	April 13 to May 12
2022	April 2 to May 1

Picture Glossary

celebrate

to do something fun on a special day

dates

a sweet fruit that grows on trees

gifts

items people give to each other on holidays

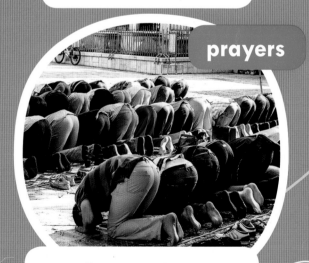

prayers

words people say or think to their god

Index

Read More

Bullard, Lisa. *Rashad's Ramadan and Eid al-Fitr.* Minneapolis: Millbrook Press, 2012.

Lawrence, Ellen. *Celebrations and Special Days.* New York: Ruby Tuesday Books, 2015.

McKissack, Fredrick, Jr. *Ramadan: Count and Celebrate!* Berkeley Heights, NJ: Enslow Publishers, 2009.

Photo Credits